C000085147

The
Viking Ship

The British Museum

The
Viking Ship

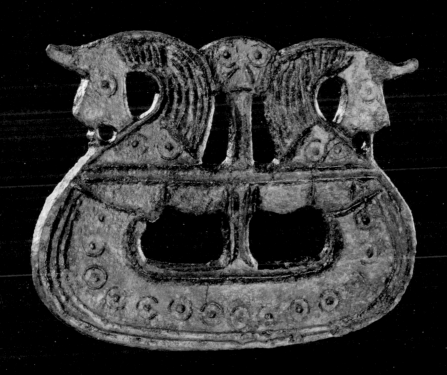

Gareth Williams

© 2014 The Trustees of the British Museum

Gareth Williams has asserted his right to be identified as the author of this work.

First published in 2014 by The British Museum Press
A division of The British Museum Company Ltd
38 Russell Square, London WC1B 3QQ
britishmuseum.org/publishing

A catalogue reference for this book is available
from the British Library.

ISBN 978-0-7141-2340-0

Designed by Grade Design
Printed and bound in Italy by Rotolito Lombarda Spa

Papers used by The British Museum Press are recyclable products made
from wood grown in well-managed forests and other controlled sources.
The manufacturing processes conform to the environmental regulations
of the country of origin.

Several of the objects illustrated in this book are from the collection
of the British Museum. Museum registration numbers are listed on pp. 94–5.
Further information about the collection can be found at britishmuseum.org

Contents

Visual glossary

1. yard
2. fore-stay
3. vane
4. stem/prow
5. knee
6. bite
7. mast partner
8. mast
9. shrouds
10. strake
11. thwart
12. gunwale
13. oar hole
14. keel
15. steering oar
16. stern
17. stringer
18. rib
19. back-stay
20. sail

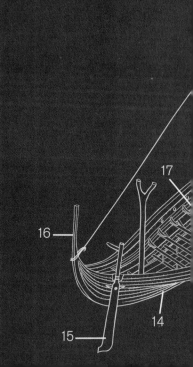

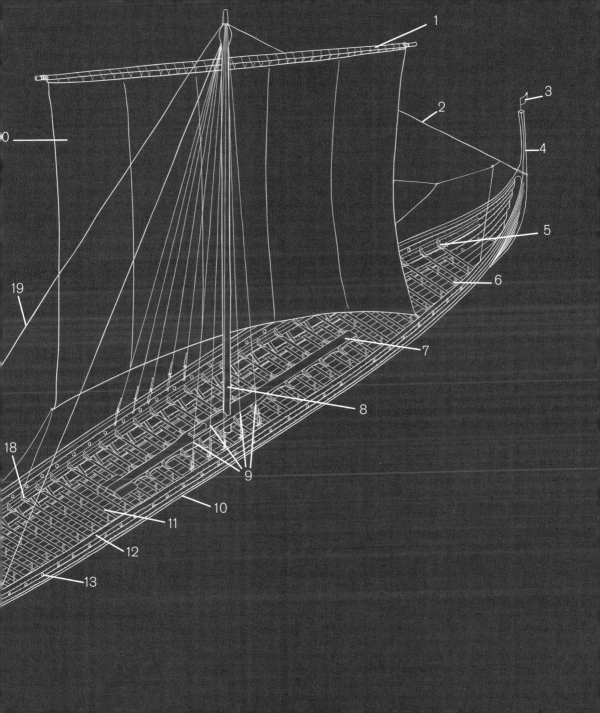

Ships, symbols and society

Men will quake with terror
Before the seventy sea-oars
Are given deserved respite
From the labours of the ocean.
Norwegian arms are driving
This iron-studded dragon
Down the storm-tossed river
Like an eagle with wings flapping.

Þjóðólfr Arnórsson, 11th century

T he ship is one of the dominant images of the Vikings. Their maritime character, along with their skills as shipbuilders and seamen, was central to the overseas exploration, trading, raiding, conquest and settlement that characterize the Viking Age (c. AD 800–1050). However, as with horned helmets, later portrayals of Viking ships are often highly inaccurate and coloured by the Romantic imagination of the nineteenth century.

The first relatively complete surviving Viking ship was not found until 1880, in a burial mound at Gokstad, southern Norway (see pp. 52–5). It was unusually well preserved due to the clay in which it was buried (fig. 1) and a replica was created in 1892 to commemorate the 400th anniversary of the crossing of the Atlantic by Christopher Columbus. The following year the replica sailed to

1. The Gokstad ship in the process of excavation, 1880.

Found in a burial mound at Gokstad farm in Sandar, Sandefjord, Vestfold, Norway.

America and was displayed at the Chicago World's Fair (fig. 2), attracting thousands of visitors. It provided a reminder that Viking ships had crossed the Atlantic almost 500 years before Columbus, highlighting the extraordinary achievements of the Viking Age.

The discovery of the Gokstad ship and the voyage of the replica caught the public imagination. Since then, many more vessels have been discovered in Scandinavia and in areas of Viking settlement abroad. The finds have been in various states of preservation and demonstrate clearly that there was no single model of 'Viking ship', but rather a variety of types developed over time for different purposes, which share a common shipbuilding tradition. Together with practical experiments using reconstructions and replicas, these finds have steadily increased our understanding of the many forms of ship and boat that existed in the Viking Age, as well as how they were built, sailed and rowed.

Even before the discovery of the Gokstad ship, a number of images from the Viking Age gave an idea of what Viking ships might

2. The *Viking*, a reconstruction based on the Gokstad ship, at the Chicago World's Fair in 1893.

VENIT · AD PEVENE □ SÆ :·

3. Invasion fleet from the Bayeaux Tapestry, 1070s. Probably Kent, England.

Embroidery (wool on linen), L *c.* 70 m
Museé de la Tapisserie de Bayeaux, Bayeaux

have looked like. These include pictures on coins, stone carvings and manuscripts, as well as the famous Bayeux Tapestry, which shows the fleet in which the Normans sailed to England prior to the conquest of 1066 (fig. 3). Modern images of Viking ships reflect a number of features found in these early illustrations: long, low sides rising to high curved stems (the archetypal 'longship'); decorated prows in the shape of dragon heads and other beasts; a single square sail; a steering oar, or *styrisbord*, on the right-hand side (hence the modern term 'starboard' for the right side of the ship) rather than a stern rudder; and often a row of shields placed along

4. (left) Norwegian 20-krone coin, 2007, with design based on the Oseberg ship.

Diam. 2.75 cm

(right) In 1969 the five Northern Postal Administrations issued stamps to mark Nordic postal cooperation with a common motif based on a Danish coin of the 9th century by Swedish designer Sven Ake Gustaffson.

H 2.5 cm, W 3.1 cm

the gunwale. Sometimes, these features are exaggerated so that the overall appearance bears little resemblance to a genuine ship, but is nevertheless immediately recognizable as a 'Viking ship'. Other modern representations are based more directly on specific models, such as the distinctively shaped Oseberg ship (see pp. 48–52).

Modern images of Viking ships

In modern times, images of Viking ships have been used in a variety of ways, but particularly as symbols of national and cultural identity. The Viking Age was the period in which the countries of Denmark, Norway and Sweden emerged as a result of the unification of several smaller kingdoms under strong royal authority. It was also a time when all three of these countries had considerable influence overseas. Recently, there has been a reaction in some parts of society in the Nordic countries against identifying so heavily with the Viking Age, rather than with contemporary achievements and developments. Nevertheless, Viking imagery is and has been utilized extensively to evoke a sense of past glory, and the iconic Viking ship lends itself to this, appearing over the years on a variety of coins, banknotes and postage stamps from the three Nordic countries (fig. 4).

The Viking ship has also been exploited to project a sense of Scandinavian identity further afield. The Sino-Scandinavian Bank, a Chinese bank with Norwegian partners that operated briefly in the 1920s, issued banknotes featuring a stylized Viking ship on one side and the Great Wall of China on the other. This juxtaposition says something about the iconic status of the Viking ship (fig. 5). However, if the Viking ship could stand as a symbol for the whole of Scandinavia in a Chinese context, it could also serve the same purpose in a more ominous context closer to home. The National Socialist Party in Germany under Adolf Hitler promoted idealized pan-Germanic unity, and while many in Denmark and Norway resisted German invasion during the Second World War, others were encouraged to join German forces, based on an appeal to common heritage and the shared threat of Soviet Russia. Recruiting posters for the SS in Scandinavia used Viking ships and other Viking imagery combined with pictures of contemporary German soldiers to suggest a sense of shared identity and purpose, as well as drawing on the Vikings' martial reputation.

5. 5-yuan note from the Sino-Scandinavian Bank, China.

Printed paper, H 8.2 cm, W 11.5 cm
British Museum, London

Not all uses of Viking ships have been on such a grand scale. They feature in a variety of company logos and branding, both in Scandinavia and elsewhere. These usually relate to either the cultural identity or perceived aspects of the character of the Vikings and their ships: speed, strength, endurance and masculinity. Cultural identity is well illustrated by the large number of different designs for tinned fish, a traditional Norwegian food, that feature Viking ships on their colourful labels (fig. 6), while identification with the character of Viking ships is probably best represented by the logo of Rover cars (fig. 7). Viking ships also serve as brand images or logos for items as diverse as beer, cognac, universities, airlines, fertilizer and luxury river cruises. The last of these is perhaps the most appropriate, since the name and logo of Viking River Cruises reminds us of the importance of Viking ships in establishing trade routes along the rivers of eastern Europe, a development that brought the Vikings into regular contact with the Byzantine empire and Islamic Caliphate in the Middle East and Central Asia.

6. Label for 'The Viking's Sardines', 1913, manufactured in Stavanger. Stavanger, the historic centre of the Norwegian sardine industry, lies in south-western Norway from where many of the early Viking raids were launched.

A maritime society

The ship was central to society within the Viking homelands (fig. 8). Apart from the Jutland peninsula, Denmark comprises a series of islands, linked until recently only by the sea (there are now connecting bridges). For periods during the Viking Age, Danish rulers also controlled much of Norway and southern Sweden, with the sea being the only link here too. Norway – the name is generally thought to come from the Old Norse for the 'Northern Way' or 'Northern sailing route' – is effectively one long coastline, with islands offshore and habitable land spread along the coast and sides of the many fjords that pierce deep into the otherwise mountainous interior. While historically Sweden has had slightly

7. Rover car logo incorporating the image of a Viking ship. The Viking ship prow and sail first appeared on the Rover radiator badge in 1929.

8. Satellite view of Scandinavia. From this perspective the maritime character of the Viking homelands is clear.

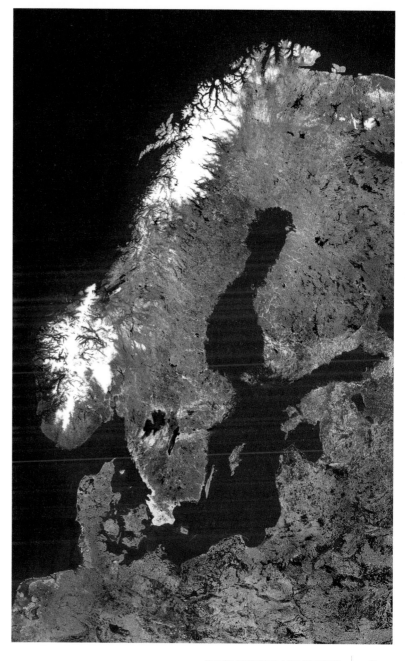

9. Ship graffito, 10th–11th century. Winetavern Street, Dublin, Ireland.

Stone. H 31 cm, W 25.5 cm
National Museum of Ireland, Dublin

better conditions for internal land travel, it also has offshore islands and navigable rivers, and even here it was much quicker and easier to cover lengthy distances by sea than by land. The chronicler Adam of Bremen, writing in the eleventh century, notes that it was possible to travel by ship from southern Sweden to Sigtuna on Lake Mälaren in eastern Sweden in five days, while the same journey overland would take a month. Ships and boats were key to communications within Scandinavia well before the Viking Age, bringing together the disparate communities in times of both war and peace.

The use of ships encouraged the development of trade both internally and externally and facilitated the gradual unification of kingdoms that were geographically fragmented, as well as enabling coastal and (by the end of the Viking Age) deep-sea fishing. The landscape of Viking and pre-Viking Scandinavia has considerable archaeological evidence of coastal settlement, including farms and lordly residences, but also a large number of small sites involved in production and trade, and a handful of major trading centres, such as Ribe and Hedeby in Denmark, Kaupang in southern Norway and Birka in Sweden. In addition, place names often refer to boats, ships, harbours and portages (places where ships are carried over land).

Ships also connected the Vikings with a number of different cultures spanning four continents, from eastern Canada in the west to Afghanistan and Uzbekistan in the east, and from the Arctic Circle to North Africa. Specialized ship types developed so that, in addition to those suitable for short journeys around and across the Baltic and the North Sea, there were lighter, shallower vessels capable of penetrating deep inland up the rivers of both eastern and western Europe, and larger deep-sea vessels capable of crossing the Atlantic. In such a maritime society it is not surprising that we have many representations of ships and boats dating from the Viking Age itself. These range from the casual – graffiti (fig. 9) and toy or model boats for children – to the more formal, such as the stylized longships shown on some of the earliest Danish coins (fig. 10). The design was borrowed from the neighbouring Frankish empire, where ship designs featured on coins minted in the major trading ports of Dorestad (modern Netherlands) and Quentovic (modern France), but the images on some of the Danish coins are subtly altered to illustrate distinctive Viking ships, with high, curved stems and a row of shields along the side. This was probably a conscious statement

10. Silver penny with ship design, probably minted in Hedeby, Denmark, early 9th century.

Hollanæs, Lolland, Denmark
Silver, 0.85 g
National Museum of Denmark, Copenhagen

about the importance of the newly established Danish trading centre of Hedeby and the strength of the fleets that defended it.

Most striking of all are the illustrations of ships on the picture stones on the island of Gotland, which show not just the shape of the ships but details of the rigging and equipment (fig. 11). It is likely that the images symbolize the transition from one world to another after death. The stones often feature a ship (usually recognizable as a warship) together with an armed man being greeted at the doors of Valhöll (Valhalla), the Hall of the Slain, where the greatest warriors were chosen by the gods for an afterlife of feasting and fighting ready for the great battle at the end of time. The Gotland stones are memorial stones, used instead of physical ship burials. However, ships were employed in a variety of ways in Viking burials and funerals, including the archetypal burning of the deceased in his ship, the marking out of symbolic ship shapes with stones around the grave, and actual burial in ships and boats. This last is particularly important for our understanding of Viking ships today because, as explored in the next chapter, some of the best surviving evidence for Viking ships and boats comes from such burials.

11. Picture stone, showing ship with Oseberg-style curved stems, 9th–10th century. Tjängvide, Alskog parish, Gotland, Sweden.

Limestone, H 174 cm
National Historical Museum, Stockholm

Burials, blockades and wrecks

The Æsir took Baldr's body, and carried it to the sea. *Hringhorni* is the name of Baldr's ship: it was greatest of all ships; the gods wished to launch it, and to set Baldr's funeral pyre thereon ... Then Baldr's body was borne out to the ship; and when his wife Nanna Nepsdottir saw that, then [her heart] burst with grief, and she died; she was borne to the pyre, and a fire lit.

Snorri Sturluson, 'Gylfaginning' in *The Prose Edda*, c. 1220

Burials

Viking ships and boats, in varying degrees of preservation, have been found in Scandinavia, France, Scotland, Ireland and the Isle of Man, and related but distinct types in England, Germany, the Netherlands and around the Baltic. These have been discovered in different contexts including some deliberately buried on land or purposely sunk in coastal areas, and others that appear to be chance losses.

The best preserved ships come from burials, as they were usually interred intact, whereas wrecks and ships sunk for blockades are typically more fragmentary. However, the state of preservation varies considerably depending on the soil type. In very rare cases most of the actual timbers survive, a tribute to the clay of southern Norway. In others the timbers are gone but the iron clench nails remain, together with a ghostly outline of the vessel in the earth (fig. 12, right).

The custom of boat burial goes back long before the Viking Age and was shared with other peoples in northern Europe, including the Anglo-Saxons, who originated in southern Scandinavia and the neighbouring areas before migrating to England. There are strong parallels, for example, between the famous Anglo-Saxon ship burial at Sutton Hoo from the early seventh century and boat graves of a similar date at Vendel and Välsgärde in eastern Sweden. Boat burials seem to have been reserved for people of relatively high status, reflecting the value of boats and ships: not everyone could afford to dispose of a ship when burying their dead. It has been suggested that the scale of some of the ship burials, including Gokstad, Oseberg and Borre in Norway, and Ladby and Hedeby in Denmark (the latter is now in Germany), indicates that the individuals buried there were royal. Smaller boat burials, while less richly furnished, nevertheless often contain expensive weapons and jewellery, again pointing to high rank if not necessarily royalty. Other burials have no actual ship, but have the shape of a ship or boat marked out in stones (fig. 13). This may signal a lower social position, symbolizing a ship for those who could not afford to bury one, or it may simply be a different burial practice. The royal enclosure and burial centre at Jelling in Denmark appears to have included a large stone ship-setting, although this was the burial place of the most powerful dynasty in Scandinavia in the late Viking Age.

The Vikings were not a single people with completely standardized practices, so some variation around the theme of ship burial is to be expected. Another alternative to burial was the burning of ships, a popular idea with film makers and still commemorated in the annual Up-Helly-Aa festival in the former Viking settlement of Shetland (fig. 14). Ship cremations are difficult to observe archaeologically, but do appear in Norse mythology, for

12. (previous page) Viking ship burial from Ladby, Denmark, early 10th century (see pp. 59–60). The remains of the ship have been left *in situ* and a museum built around them.

13. Boat-shaped stone setting from the Viking-Age cemetery at Lindolm Høje, near Ålborg, Denmark.

14. The burning of the 'galley', a stylized Viking ship, forms a central part of the Up-Helly-Aa festival in Lerwick, Shetland each January.

example in the story of the death of the god Baldr, who was cremated in his ship *Hringhorni* along with his wife Nanna and a dwarf who was accidentally kicked into the flames. The story has some parallels with an account by the tenth-century Arab traveller Ahmad ibn Fadlān, who describes the funeral of a chieftain of the Rūs (usually interpreted as partly or wholly of Scandinavian origin) on the Volga *c.* 922. In this account the chieftain was cremated in his ship along with a slave girl who was sacrificed so that she could accompany her master. This is consistent with the presence in the boat burial of a wealthy man at Balladoole, Isle of Man, of a female skeleton showing signs of a violent death.

Both the mythological and the historical accounts of ship cremations suggest that these were public spectacles, and the same is likely to be true of ship burials, with the dead and their treasures laid out for view before the grave was covered over. One interpretation of ship burials is that the ship is there to convey the deceased to the afterlife, and this can be supported by graves containing other means of transport, including female graves with the upper parts of wagons as coffins, and male graves with horses. Occasionally these might be combined with ship burials, as with the presence of four sleighs and a wagon in the Oseberg burial (fig. 15), or several horses in the Ladby burial. Alternatively the ship, along with the other grave goods, may be seen as a symbol of the deceased's wealth and power. The timber, iron, textiles and manpower required to build and outfit a ship (see pp. 34–9) usually made it the most valuable item in the grave. A third interpretation is that the ship is a sacrifice to the gods.

Apart from Baldr's *Hringhorni*, two other ships of note appear in Norse mythology. The *Naglfar*, purportedly made of the fingernails and toenails of the dead, ferried the forces of the giants (enemies

15. Wagon with decorative carving from the Oseberg ship, buried *c.* 834. Oseberg, Sem, Vestfold, Norway.

Museum of Cultural History, University of Oslo, Oslo

of the gods) to the battle of Ragnarök at the end of the world, and ship burial might plausibly be linked with such a vessel of death. However, a more likely association is with *Skiðblaðnir*, a magical ship connected in different traditions to Odin, the chief of the gods, and Frey, the god of fertility, who was also strongly identified with the sea. Stone ship-settings might act as a symbolic replacement for a real ship in any of these interpretations, even the display of wealth, since those attending the funeral would be well aware of whether the dead man or woman had an actual ship of corresponding size.

VÆRING
ENEBERETTIGET 1904

Whatever the reasons behind ship burials, they have left us with some of the finest surviving examples of Viking ships, and in some cases also with a great assortment of grave objects, although robbers in the past often stripped the sites of precious metal items. Unfortunately, this is true of one of the most elaborate ship burials, from *c.* 834, at Oseberg, southern Norway, which was discovered in 1904 (fig. 16, left). Despite this, it is remarkable for the decorative carving on the stems of the ship and on the sleighs, the wagon (see fig. 15) and the four decorative animal-headed posts (the purpose of which remains uncertain) that were buried with the ship, as well as a decorated bucket (probably from Ireland) and a range of textiles, including a beautiful tapestry. The grave contained two women, one in her eighties and the other in her fifties. The relationship between them is uncertain and it is not clear whose was the primary burial in the grave, but DNA analysis of the older skeleton suggests family origins in the Middle East, probably in Iran, a reminder of the long-distance contacts already opened up by Viking ships by the early ninth century.

At Gokstad, not far from Oseberg, another burial was discovered. This had been even more thoroughly robbed of portable items, but in addition to the well-preserved ship, with a row of shields along each of its sides, it contained three smaller boats, one with six oars and two with four each. The burial chamber, placed in the centre of the ship, and what appears to be the frame for either a tent or an awning to cover the deck area of the ship, were also found in the excavation. Recent archaeological investigations indicate that the burial took place close to a hitherto unknown major settlement, providing a parallel to the Hedeby ship burial (see p. 28). Other burials in southern Norway include the ship from Tune (see p. 55) and a mound cemetery at Borre. The first Viking ship recorded in modern times was discovered at Borre in 1852 and, although the ship itself was poorly preserved, the decorated artefacts in the grave gave their name to the 'Borre' style of ornamentation.

The so-called 'boat-chamber grave' buried outside the walls of the Viking town of Hedeby, on the southern border of Denmark, is also better known for the objects buried with it, including two swords, than for the ship itself, which is poorly preserved. However, the grave is interesting in two respects relating to ships. Firstly, the main chamber was under the ship, which was less common than placing it in the ship itself, although there are parallels elsewhere. Secondly, both stems of the ship are missing, as is most of the mast, but the ship was buried with the mast in place. Therefore, the upper part of the mast and both stems may have projected out of the mound.

16. (previous page) Excavation of the Oseberg ship in 1904.

17. Sword found at the Ardamurchan boat burial, Scotland.

Iron with silver and copper alloy. L *c.* 75 cm

18. Detail of the pommel of the sword found at the Ardamurchan boat burial, Scotland.

The sword, which dates from the 10th century, is of an unusual style, as the shapes of the pommel and the lower guard would not normally be found together – although the ornamentation indicates that they were made as a pair. The sword may be a Frankish import from Continental Europe, or possibly a Viking adaptation of Frankish styles.

In 2011, a Viking boat burial was discovered at Port an Eilean Mhòir in Ardnamurchan, Scotland (figs 17–18). Only the rivets (some with small fragments of wood still attached) survive from the boat itself, but these are enough to indicate its approximate size and shape, that is, around 5 metres long by 1.5 metres wide. The boat contained a male grave, equipped with weapons, including an expensive sword probably imported from Continental Europe, as well as a whetstone from Norway and a brooch from Ireland or the Irish Sea, pointing to the range of contacts offered by Viking boats and ships. Boat burials of this kind represent a step down the social ladder from 'royal' burials such as at Oseberg and Hedeby, but still demonstrate the wealth and power of the deceased, who was probably a local chieftain. Other examples are recorded from the Northern and Western Isles of Scotland and the Isle of Man, and these usually seem to have been individuals of comparable status.

Blockades

Not all of the known Viking ships come from burial mounds. One of the most dramatic excavations of ship remains followed a chance discovery in 1957 by sport divers in the Peberrenden channel near Skuldelev, a few kilometres north of Roskilde in Denmark, an important town of the late Viking Age. In 1962 the area of the Roskilde Fjord immediately around the ships was dammed and drained to permit their excavation (fig. 19). It quickly became clear that the ships had been deliberately placed to form a blockade as part of a network of defences to impede potential attackers sailing up the fjord to Roskilde. The blockade was built in at least three phases: a first phase in the 1060s, including the ships Skuldelev 1, 3 and 5 (see pp. 60–3, 77–81); a second phase in the 1070s, with Skuldelev 2 and 6 (see pp. 67, 74–7); and a third phase of uncertain date when the barrier was reinforced with vertical poles.

A similar blockade was partially excavated in 1982–3, protecting the harbour of Foteviken in southern Sweden. Here a barrier was initially created from stone and timber, and later reinforced by pulling ships laden with stones down to the water, then sinking them on top of the existing barrier. A gap was left in the middle of the blockade through which friendly vessels were permitted to pass, but this was eventually filled by another ship being dragged across. The blockade probably dates from the early twelfth century and the ships within it from the very end of the eleventh century, so they are not discussed in detail in this book. They do, however, help to show the continuity of the Viking shipbuilding tradition at the end of the Viking Age.

19. Excavation of the Skuldelev ships from Roskilde Fjord in 1962.

20. The Äskekärr ship, late 10th century.

Oak, L *c.* 16 m.
Göteborgs Museum

Wrecks

For all the shipbuilding skill of the Vikings, their ships were still vulnerable to rough seas and bad weather. A cargo ship that sank around the year 1000 was found at Klåstad in southern Norway (see p. 79). Although originally lost at sea, it was left landlocked by the shifting coastline in the area. Another cargo ship of the same date seems to have been a chance loss at Äskekärr on the River Göta (fig. 20, and see p. 77), while wrecks have also been recovered from the harbour areas of the Danish towns of Roskilde and Hedeby, including the largest Viking warship found to date: Roskilde 6 (see pp. 67–73). Another warship from Hedeby (see p. 64) perhaps offers a counterpart to the ships that ended their working lives as parts of blockades. It shows signs of scorching above the waterline and may have been sent in as a fireship to burn the harbour at Hedeby before eventually sinking.

The construction and evolution of Viking ships

Thorbergr skavhǫgg (Shave-Stroke) is the name given to the man who was the stem-builder of the ship, but there were many others involved: some to fell [timber], some to carve it, some forging nails, some carrying timber. All the parts were constructed with great precision. The ship was both long and broad and high-sided and large-timbered.

Heimskringla, Snorri Sturluson, *c.* 1230

Building the Viking ship

The ships mentioned so far differ considerably in size and shape. This reflects regional variations in shipbuilding across the Viking world; the development over time of specialized ship types for a range of functions; the different levels of wealth and resources available to shipbuilders and their patrons; and chance survival. There may well be other varieties that have not yet been found, but all of these ships follow broadly the same shipbuilding tradition.

Viking ships were what is known as clinker-built. Unlike some other types of shipbuilding, where the main strength of the ship is in its frame, which is built first and to which the strakes (or planks) are subsequently attached, in clinker building the strakes are affixed first to create a hollow shell and internal supports are added later (fig. 21). In clinker-built ships, the strength is in the hull and the internal supports are relatively insubstantial. Overall the

21. The mains stages of construction of a Viking ship, based on the warship Skuldelev 2 (see pp. 64–7).

1. Carefully shaped stems are fastened to each end of the keel.

2. The lower strakes (planks) are built up to either side of the keel and stems.

3. Floor timbers are fastened across the lower strakes to support the shape of the lower hull. The keelson is placed onto the keel, ready to hold the mast, then the upper strakes are added.

4. Stringers are added for support along the length of the hull. Ribs and knees support each side, while crossbeams known as bites and the thwarts (rowing benches) above them lock the sides together.

5. Oar holes are cut into one of the upper strakes. The mast partner and deck boards are fitted. The steering oar is added on the right-hand side of the stern. The mast, yard and sail are stepped and rigged.

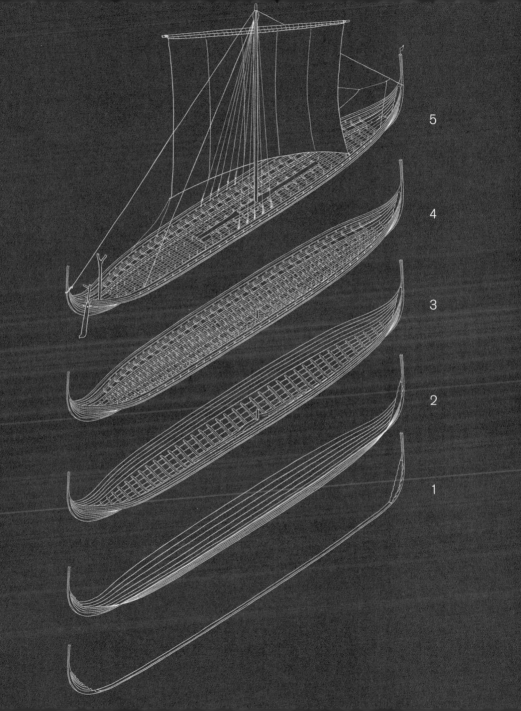

5

4

3

2

1

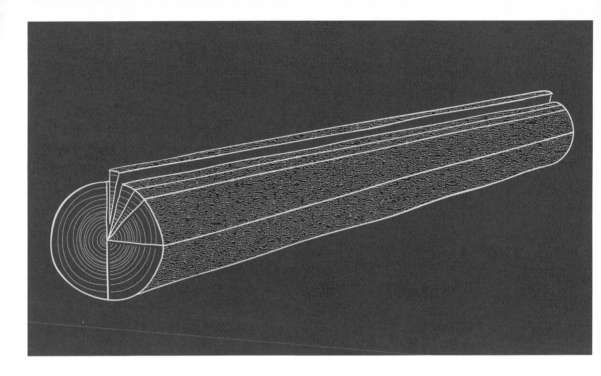

vessel is therefore light and flexible for its size and it is this rather than a heavy internal skeleton that enables it to resist the pressure of the sea and minor collisions. The flexibility was aided by the fact that the strakes were normally cut radially along the grain, rather than cutting across the grain (fig. 22), so that the vessel benefited from the natural pliability of the timber. This may have been deliberate, or simply a result of the technique used to carve the planks, whereby the logs were first split with wedges and then shaped with axes and adzes instead of saws. While large straight trees were ideal for the keel and the strakes, naturally curved timbers were preferable for the stems and the internal frames, as this again made the most of the strength of the wood by cutting along the grain.

22. The radial cutting of wedges from a log. These wedges could then be trimmed into planks.

23. Stepped stem for a clinker-built boat, 885–1035. Found in a bog on the island of Eigg, Scotland, where it had probably been left to harden.

Oak. L 193 cm, H 30 cm
National Museums Scotland, Edinburgh

24. Clench nails from a boat burial at Lilleberge, Nord-Trøndelag, Norway, 9th–10th century.

Iron. L *c.* 2.5 cm
British Museum, London

Construction began with the keel and stems (fig. 23), which were fastened by overlapping scarf joints, strengthened with iron or wooden nails. Ideally the keel was built from a single piece of timber, but this was not always possible, especially for large ships and, although weaker, it was sometimes necessary to construct a 'pieced' keel in two or more sections. The strakes were then added, with each overlapping the one below and locked into place with iron rivets or clench nails (fig. 24). The ribs, bites, knees and thwarts reinforced the shape of the hull already determined by the strakes. These might be fastened to the strakes either with iron or wooden nails, or (in the early Norwegian ships) by lashing to cleats carved on the inside of the strakes. In some larger vessels the lower supports were inserted before the upper strakes, to prevent the hull from sagging in the course of construction. For the same reason, the internal frames on the deeper cargo ships of the late Viking Age and beyond (see pp. 74–83) tend to be much heavier and more solid than on lighter weight ships.

The ships were designed to be rowed as well as sailed. Typically they have holes for the oars, although smaller boats often have

25. Two styles of rigging shown on contemporary illustrations of Viking ships. Both show the mast supported by stays fore and aft, and shrouds to either side. Most images show just the bottom corners of the sails fastened to the sides of the ship (as on the left), but the Gotland pictures stones (see pp. 18–19) typically show a more complicated arrangement, with a series of ropes along the bottom edge of the sail (as on the right). These may have offered more precise control over the angle of the sail.

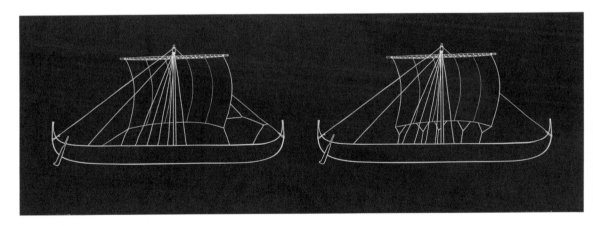

rowlocks (to keep the oars in place) above the gunwale. The only rigging used in this period seems to have been based around a single square sail, usually made of wool. Experiments with modern reconstructions show that this was quite effective, allowing ships to tack at up to 60 degrees against the wind. Most contemporary illustrations show very simple rigging, with stays supporting the mast fore and aft, and sometimes with shrouds providing lateral support. Some of the Gotland stones, however, appear to show a more complicated arrangement with multiple ropes attached to the bottom of the sail (fig. 25). Ropes were made from a variety of material, including lime bast, twisted seal and walrus hide, and horse hair. While it is rarely recorded, hemp may also have been used in the Viking Age and it later came to dominate rope making.

The ancestry of the Viking ship

The origins of the clinker-built tradition go back centuries before the Viking Age. Pictures of long, low canoes exist in a number of prehistoric rock carvings. Opinion is divided on whether these represent skin boats stretched around a wooden frame, bark boats or log boats, or indeed a mixture of these varieties. It seems likely that Scandinavian clinker building grew primarily out of a log-boat tradition, possibly with some influence from skin boats too. Log boats can be divided into two categories. In the first, the final shape of the boat is simply carved out of the log. The second is the so-called expanded log boat, in which the log is carved to shape and then, following the application of heat, the sides are bent outwards in the middle, causing the boat to be wider in the centre and the two ends to be pulled up slightly, thus creating a more obvious 'boat' shape. Like the clinker boat, this design requires some internal reinforcement, although in this case to stop it bending inwards rather than collapsing outwards. An expanded log boat can form a vessel in its own right or can be made deeper by the addition of strakes along the side.

The earliest surviving boat in the clinker-built tradition seems to represent a stage of development beyond this. In the boat from Hjortspring in Jutland, dating from *c.* 350 BC, the expanded log has been replaced by a broad, curved bottom plank, terminating in upward-extending horns. There is a stem attached to each end of the plank, just behind the horns, creating a vessel 19 metres long, with a profile reminiscent of prehistoric rock carvings (fig. 26). There are two overlapping strakes to each side of the central plank, which are sewn together rather than fastened by nails, possibly an influence from the skin-boat tradition. Lashings also attach the hull to the internal frames. Each frame consists of a thwart as a seat for a crew member, on top of a curved rib supporting the shape of the hull. There are no rowlocks or oar holes, suggesting that the boat was paddled rather than rowed, and there is no sign of a sail.

26. Reconstruction model of the Hjortspring boat, *c.* 350 BC.

National Museum of Denmark, Copenhagen

27. Reconstruction drawing of the boat from Nydam, Denmark.

A further evolutionary stage can be seen in a large boat deposited in a bog at Nydam, close to Denmark's southern border. The Nydam boat is around 23 metres long and dates from *c.* AD 320 (fig. 27). There are several technological developments that set this apart from the Hjortspring boat. The projecting lower horns have gone, leaving a single stem at either end, to which the strakes are attached, and there are more and narrower strakes to each side. These still overlap, but are fastened with iron rivets. The internal frames again have thwarts above them, but these now have rowlocks on both sides, indicating that the boat was designed to be rowed. The boat also has a single large steering oar like the later

Viking ships. However, it did not sail as there are no fittings for a mast or rigging. Although the basic construction represents a development of the clinker tradition, the improvements probably result from contacts with Roman shipbuilding traditions, as there was extensive contact between southern Scandinavia and the Roman empire in the third to the fifth centuries. The same period also saw the first recorded use of animal figureheads in northern Europe (fig. 28), again possibly owing to Roman influence, and these were the precursors of the dragon heads of later Viking ships.

Further development is represented by the ship from Sutton Hoo, in Suffolk. This is Anglo-Saxon rather than Viking, but the Anglo-Saxons had their origins in southern Scandinavia and the adjoining area, and took their shipbuilding traditions with them. The ship survives only as an approximately 27-metre-long impression in the soil and probably had a crew of forty rowers (fig. 29). It dates from the late sixth or early seventh century and has a distinct, if shallow, keel, with the strakes fastened together with iron rivets. There is no evidence of any fittings for a mast or rigging, so the ship may have been designed for rowing only. However, it is possible that traces of a keelson or other mast fittings were removed or obliterated in the creation of the burial chamber and trials of *Sae Wulfing*, a half-sized reconstruction, have shown it to be effective under sail. Fragments of another vessel of a comparable date were recovered at Gredstedbro, in southern Jutland and these are of similar size and character to the Nydam boat. Not enough has been recovered to know whether the Gredstedbro ship carried a sail, although the relatively slight construction perhaps makes it unlikely. The one feature of the ship that links it to later vessels is that the strakes were apparently fastened to the ribs with trenails (wooden pins) rather than bound with lashings. Another ship, from Kvalsund in western Norway, dating

28. Animal figurehead, 300–600, found in the River Scheldt, Belgium.

Oak. H 149 cm
British Museum, London

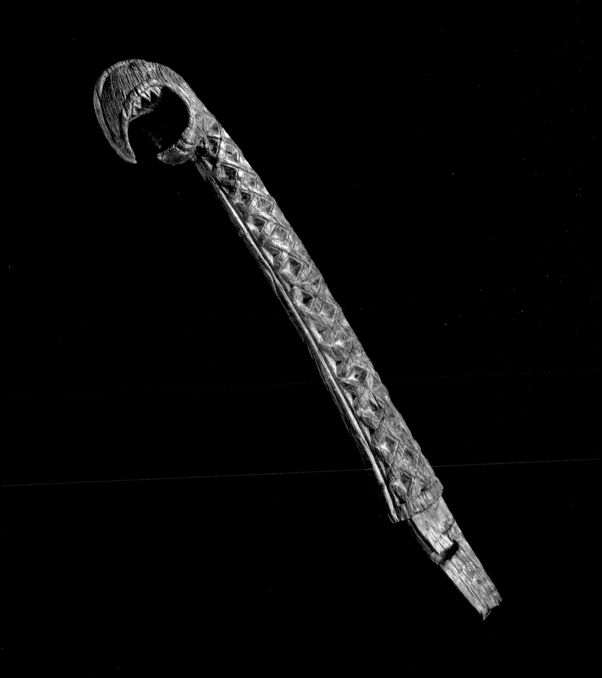

29. The excavation of the Mound 1 ship burial at Sutton Hoo, Suffolk, in 1939.

from the end of the seventh century, has a more developed keel and may have been capable of sailing, but there are no traces of any fittings for a mast and the high stems and low freeboard (height of side between waterline and deck) mean that even with its rudimentary keel it would not have been stable under sail in strong winds.

If the sail was not already in use in Scandinavia by the seventh century it was certainly introduced before the traditional beginning of the Viking Age, c. AD 800. Some of the Gotland picture stones showing sailing ships predate this, while a Scandinavian sailing ship used for a mass burial, and apparently dating from the mid-eighth century, was recently discovered at Saarema in Estonia, although full details of this ship have not yet been published. Scandinavia also had close contact with the Franks, who certainly had sails before 800. Furthermore, many of the initial Viking raids on Britain and Ireland originated in western Norway. From here the obvious route is directly across the North Sea rather than along the southern coastal route and it is unlikely, though not impossible, that such voyages were routinely undertaken with oars alone.

In this context it is interesting that the earliest surviving ship that can be categorized as a Viking ship was built in western Norway, although it was found further east. This is the Oseberg ship, built in c. 820; and from then until the end of the Viking Age there are a number of vessels that demonstrate the continued evolution of Scandinavian ship design. However, the picture is not entirely clear, as all of the better preserved ships up to c. 900 come from Norway, whereas later ships come from Denmark, Norway and Sweden, so it is possible that the former represent a regional variation rather than an evolutionary stage. Nevertheless, current evidence suggests that ships up to c. 900 were typically multi-purpose vessels, with sufficient crew to act as warships, but broad and deep enough to carry cargo (see pp. 48–55). The tenth and eleventh centuries saw the development of more specialized ships for use either as warships or cargo ships, while size of ships also increased in this period (see pp. 56–83).

Several words for ship survive in Old Norse, but it is not clear that these were necessarily used to indicate distinctive ship types, although they have sometimes been interpreted in this way by archaeologists. Most of the early references come from poetry and the choice of word may be inspired more by poetic structures (alliteration was an important element in Viking poetry) than by strict attention to ship typology. The most common word is *skip*, which, like modern English, can be qualified by a descriptive element, such as *langskip* (longship), *herskip* (warship) or *kaupskip* (trading ship). The term *skeið* (pl. *skeiðr* or *skeiðar*) is usually only used where a warship

30. Vanes like this were originally used as figureheads for ships although surviving examples, including this one, were later reused as wind vanes on churches.

Weather vane, 1000–1050, Heggen Church, Buskerud, Norway.

Gilt copper, brass. L 28 cm, H 29 cm
Museum of Cultural History, University of Oslo, Oslo

31. Wooden stick with carving of a fleet, 13th century. The carving includes some ships with dragon-head prows and others with what appear to be metal vanes (see fig. 30).

Juniper. L *c.* 25 cm
University Museum of Bergen, Bergen

is implied, as is the term *snekkja* (pl. *snekkjur*). In some cases the context suggests that the *skeið* was bigger than the *snekkja*, but in others both words describe the same vessel, so this is not a clear distinction. Similarly, *dreki* (pl. *drekar*), meaning 'dragon', sometimes, but not exclusively, refers to large ships and is probably just a poetic metaphor for a ship rather than a ship type, although it may be inspired by the use of dragon heads on ships' prows (figs 30–1).

The term *knörr* or *knarr* (pl. *knerrir*) is often borrowed by archaeologists to denote a cargo ship, but its meaning in the Viking Age is more ambiguous. Some references support this, but others equally clearly allude to warships. A common feature may be that *knerrir* were ocean-going ships of a broader, deeper construction than other vessels and therefore more likely to be cargo ships (see pp. 80–3). Another term, *karfi*, has sometimes been taken to denote a high-status vessel, almost the equivalent of a modern royal yacht, but this term is on one occasion used of a ship also described as a *hlaegiskip* ('ridicule ship'), so the assumption that it implies status must be regarded with caution.

The early Viking ships

'The wind is sharp tonight, it tosses the white hair of the sea,
I do not fear the crossing of the Clear Sea [Irish Sea],
by the wild warriors of Lothlind [Vikings].'

Anonymous Irish Monk, mid-9th century

Current evidence suggests that ships in the early Viking Age were to some extent general purpose ships: fast and agile enough to be effective for raiding, but with the capacity to carry a limited cargo. Ships for small-scale raiding and trading often had similar requirements. Raiders needed sufficient space for supplies and for loot, which might include slaves and livestock as well as smaller treasures, while traders had to have a large enough crew to defend themselves against pirates. Indeed, the same people may have acted as raiders and traders on different occasions. This ambiguity may explain the events of one of the earliest recorded raids, in Dorset. A royal official and his men were killed by three shiploads of Vikings, apparently having approached them, according to *Æthelweard's Chronicle*, 'because he thought they were traders'.

32. The Oseberg ship, *c.* 820, with some of the finds from the ship burial in the background.

Oak. L 21.5 m
Viking Ship Museum, Oslo

The Oseberg ship

Of the three surviving early Norwegian ships, the oldest is from Oseberg in Vestfold. The ship was constructed in western Norway *c.* 820 from oak. Analysis of the burial chamber indicates that it was

33. The highly decorated stem of the Oseberg ship terminates in a stylized serpent's head. The 'dragons' of Norse mythology sometimes appear as giant serpents rather than the winged quadrupeds more familiar from modern imagery, so this can be seen as a variant on other 'dragon' figureheads (see pp. 46–7).

buried *c.* 834 (fig. 32). It is approximately 21.5 metres long, with fifteen oar holes to either side, plus a steering oar, and therefore required a crew of thirty-one. The ship was designed to be sailed as well as rowed and visible repairs to the mast partner show that it had sailed at least once. Although it had partly collapsed under the weight of the soil before it was found in 1904, around 95 per cent of the original timbers survived and the ship was reconstructed into the current form in 1906–7. It has high curving stems, but drops to a low, shallow profile amidships, with little freeboard and not much depth below the waterline.

There are elaborate carvings on both the stem and the stern of the Oseberg ship (fig. 33). The rounded terminals on the stems have been reconstructed based on illustrations on coins and the Gotland picture stones (see pp. 18–19). The intricate decoration indicates that the ship belonged to someone of high, or even royal, status. However, the low lines mean that the ship as currently displayed is not particularly stable and would be extremely vulnerable in rough seas. The relatively small size of the mast partner and keelson and the fact that the mast partner had required repair suggest that these would have been too weak to support the pressure of the mast in high wind. This, coupled with the rather unsuccessful sailing trials of modern reconstructions, could imply that the Oseberg ship was not a true sea-going vessel, but something more like a royal yacht, suitable only for looking impressive when cruising along the coast.

Developments in technology and experience gained in the conservation and interpretation of several other Viking ships mean that today's ship conservators are able to undertake more informed analysis of the original timbers. New research from 2006 onwards has concluded that the shape of the Oseberg ship would have been deeper and more rounded amidships, and tank tests of a model suggest that it would have been more stable in the water than the vessels based on the lines proposed in 1906–7. A new reconstruction has recently been completed at Tønsberg, in southern Norway (close to the place where the Oseberg ship was found) and there are plans to test its sailing abilities on the open sea as well as in coastal waters. If this reinterpretation is correct, the Oseberg ship may well be more representative of early Viking ships than was previously thought. The size is comparable with documentary evidence suggesting crews of thirty to forty men, while the deeper, more rounded shape would mean a greater capacity for stores, loot or cargo below the removable deck, increasing the ship's suitability for raiding and trading overseas. The fact that the ship is comparatively short and also has a shallow draft makes it ideal for the journeys up major rivers widely recorded of Viking fleets in the ninth century.

The Gokstad ship

If there are doubts over the seaworthiness of the Oseberg ship, this is not the case with the ship from Gokstad, also in Vestfold (see also pp. 8–9). This ship (fig. 34) has been dated to the 890s and was buried *c.* 910. Also made of oak, the ship is 23.24 metres long, with sixteen oar holes on either side. The ship thus required a crew of thirty-three men, although the relatively wide hull meant that there was room for around double this number. The profile of the Gokstad ship is deeper and rounder than the Oseberg ship, with a higher freeboard. Although the oar holes are not placed in the uppermost strake but in the third strake from the top, these are slotted to make it easier to take out the oars. There are removable shutters to cover the oar holes when under sail, so helping the ship to cope with heavy seas (fig. 35). Despite the attention paid to the design of the oar holes, there are no permanent rowing benches and it is likely

34. The Gokstad ship, *c.* 895, fully restored. The slightly lighter-coloured timbers are modern replacements, but the rest of the ship is original.

Oak, iron. L 23.24 m
Viking Ship Museum, Oslo

GOKSTADSKIBET

35. Internal details of the Gokstad ship. The mast partner in the centre of the photograph sits directly above the keelson, providing additional support to hold the mast in place. In the background it is possible to see some of the shutters, which could be used to block the oar holes when these were not in use.

that the rowers sat on chests. These could be used for personal kit or cargo and had the advantage of being convenient to stow and to move to different places to adjust the sailing qualities of the ship.

The lower part of the Gokstad ship's mast survives, as well as a mast partner and keelson strong enough to take the pressure of a substantial sail (fig. 35). It is estimated that this would have been over 100 square metres in size and capable of moving the ship at up to 12 knots. A number of reconstructions of the ship have proven to be effective, even crossing the Atlantic, although it is likely that a rather different type of vessel was normally used for ocean voyages in the Viking Age (see p. 80). The slightly deeper draft of the Gokstad ship made it less suitable for very shallow waters than the Oseberg ship, but it was still highly versatile and the greater depth gave added capacity for cargo or stores. While it lacks the decorative carving of the Oseberg ship, the curving lines of the Gokstad ship have an elegance of their own, making this one of the most beautiful surviving artefacts from the Viking Age as well as a prime example of an effective multi-purpose Viking ship.

The Tune ship

The third early ship comes from Tune in Østfold in southern Norway, on the opposite side of the Oslo Fjord from Gokstad and Oseberg. It was found in 1867 and like the other two was buried in a mound, although the grave had been more comprehensively looted than the others before it was discovered. The ship is also much more poorly preserved, making it harder to reconstruct the original lines accurately. The Tune ship was built of Norwegian oak and with an estimated length of c. 18.4 metres was probably slightly shorter than either the Gokstad or Oseberg ships. There are around twelve oar holes to either side and thus the ship would have required a crew of about twenty-five. Although the mast partner and internal ribs and beams are substantial, suggesting a comparatively sturdy vessel, there are only ten surviving strakes on either side of the keel, which would make it very low and rather unseaworthy. An extra one or two strakes per side would have increased the freeboard of the ship, bringing it closer in dimensions to the new interpretation of the Oseberg ship, and also more capable of carrying a cargo as well as a crew.

EARLY 'GENERAL PURPOSE' VIKING SHIPS

Ship	Date	Length (m)	Breadth (m)	Length/breadth ratio	No. of oars
Oseberg	c. 820	21.50	5.10	4.2	30
Gokstad	c. 895	23.24	5.20	4.5	32
Tune	c. 910	c. 18.40	c. 4.35	4.2	24

Warships

Such, also, was the decoration of the ships, that ... to those who were looking from afar they seemed [to be made] more of flame than of wood ... Here shone the gleam of weapons, but there the flame of hanging shields. Gold burned on the prows, silver also shone on ships of various shapes. So great, in fact, was the appearance of the fleet, that if its lord had wished to conquer any people, the ships alone would have terrified the enemy, even before the warriors aboard could join battle.

Anon., *Encomium Emmae Reginae*, 1041–2

Viking ships are often referred to as 'longships', but the term should strictly only be applied to vessels specifically built as warships. The word is first recorded in the *Anglo-Saxon Chronicle* for 896, possibly coinciding with the development of a new type of warship that was much longer in relation to its breadth than ships such as the Gokstad ship, although these too were probably used in warfare. Whereas the Gokstad and Oseberg ships have a length to breadth ratio of 4.5:1 and 4.2:1, the true longships were much narrower in proportion (fig. 36), with a ratio of between 7:1 and 11.4:1. Therefore, there was little room for anything on board apart from the crew, personal weapons and equipment, and very limited supplies. On the one hand, this restricted the use of such ships,

36. The relative shapes of different ships. Gokstad and Oseberg are multi-purpose ships and Skuldelev 1 is a cargo ship. Skuldelev 2, Skuldelev 5 and Roskilde 6 are warships. Warships are typically low and narrow in relation to their length.

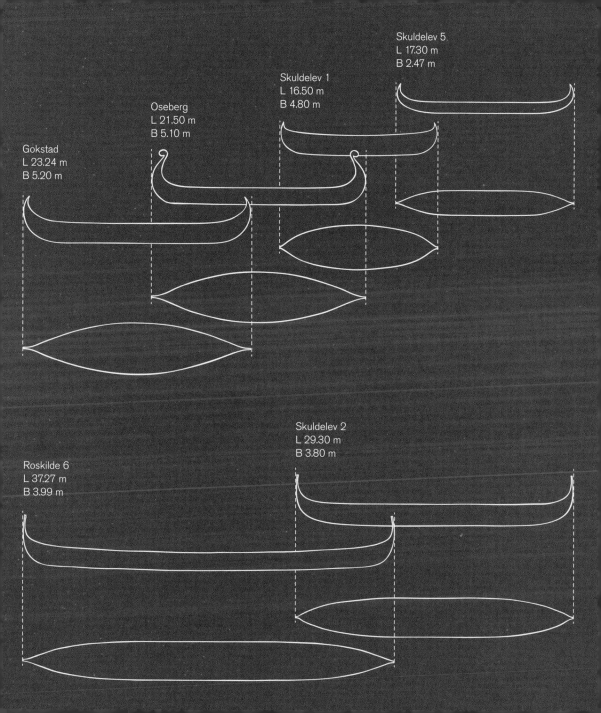

Skuldelev 5
L 17.30 m
B 2.47 m

Skuldelev 1
L 16.50 m
B 4.80 m

Oseberg
L 21.50 m
B 5.10 m

Gokstad
L 23.24 m
B 5.20 m

Skuldelev 2
L 29.30 m
B 3.80 m

Roskilde 6
L 37.27 m
B 3.99 m

as they could not undertake long voyages without being accompanied by additional supply ships, or stopping frequently to resupply. It also reduced their capacity to carry plunder. On the other hand, their narrowness made them lighter and faster than broader ships of the same length. This, combined with their substantial crews in proportion to their size, meant that they were highly manoeuvrable, at least if the crew was well disciplined. They were therefore effective transport for troops, with the warriors doubling as rowers. The large number of oars also meant that such ships were less reliant on the elements than some other sailing vessels of the period.

The design of the ships was less than ideal for actual combat and, despite the Vikings' reputation as both warriors and seamen, most battles were fought on land. The ships were unsuitable for ramming owing to their light construction (see pp. 34–6). A heavy blow directly to the prow risked forcing apart the joints between the stem and the keel, and between the stem and the strakes behind it. Battles at sea are recorded, but they seem to have been little different from land battles, with several ships being lashed together to create a larger and more stable platform, and combat commencing with an exchange of missiles such as arrows, spears, throwing axes and stones. This changed to hand-to-hand fighting as the opposing ships closed on each other. Larger, higher ships provided an advantage to their crews, in the same way that command of the upper ground offered a tactical advantage on land. Although longships shared the characteristic of being long, narrow purpose-built warships, they varied considerably in size, with bigger vessels acting both as an immediately visible reminder of the status of anyone with control of sufficient resources to build one and as a manifestation of military power.

Small warships

The oldest ship that may perhaps be considered a true longship comes from the boat-chamber grave at Hedeby. The ship is poorly preserved and its shape can be reconstructed only from the distribution of the iron rivets. The absence of surviving timber means that the ship cannot be dated precisely, but the grave goods suggest that it was buried in the middle of the ninth century. Therefore, the ship was probably made in the decades just before this and shortly after the Oseberg ship (which was c. 820). The ship had at least nine strakes to either side. It is unclear whether the timbers may have spread under the pressure of the earth before they rotted, but, allowing for this, the estimated length is 17 to 20 metres, with a length to breadth ratio of anywhere between 4.8:1 and 7.4:1. The former would indicate similar proportions to the Tune ship, with which it has some similarities, while the latter is more akin to the true longships of the tenth and eleventh centuries.

The earliest certain longship is the burial ship from Ladby (see pp. 20–2). Again, the timbers have not survived, which means that the vessel cannot be dated accurately, but as the grave is from the early tenth century, the ship must be from c. 900. The imprint and rivets show that the ship was at least 21.5 metres long, and narrow, with fifteen to sixteen oars on each side. The Ladby ship therefore required a similar minimum crew to the Oseberg and Gokstad ships, but the narrower shape would have restricted the space for additional crew members. While the keelson is no longer extant, iron rings for the attachment of the rigging demonstrate that the ship was designed for sailing as well as rowing. Iron curls from the prow and an iron band with spikes from the stern have been interpreted as decorations added to a carved wooden dragon's or lion's head and tail, with the curls representing a mane down the back of the neck, an image with parallels in a decorative mould of a dragon's head from Birka, in Sweden (fig. 37). Similar metal fittings have also been recovered from boat burials, including one at Île-de-Groix in Brittany. A carving of a fleet from Bryggen in Norway, although dating from after the Viking Age, appears to indicate that only the ships of leaders had dragon-head prows (see fig. 31) and this would fit with the evident high status of the burial, suggesting that the Ladby ship was the warship of an important local chieftain.

A very different interpretation has been placed on another small longship, which formed part of the Skuldelev blockade (see p. 30). Skuldelev 5 is 17.3 metres long, with a length to breadth ratio of

37. Decorative curls from a figurehead from the Ladby ship, early 10th century.

Iron
Vikingemuseet, Ladby

Slate mould for a dragon-head terminal, 9th–10th century.

Birka, Sweden. L 8.4 cm, W 6.6 cm
Statens Historiska Museum, Stockholm

The curls at the back of the dragon's neck on the mould indicate how the iron curls would have been used on a ship's figurehead.

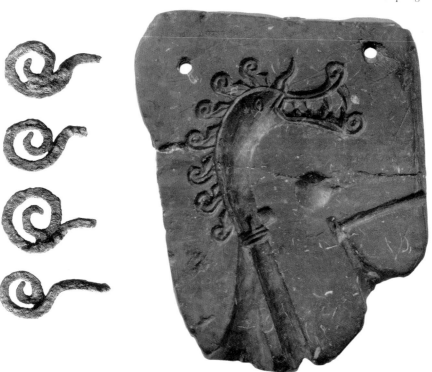

38. The warship Skuldelev 5,
c. 1030. Skuldelev, near
Roskilde, Denmark.

Oak, ash and pine. L 17.3 m
Viking Ship Museum, Roskilde

around 7:1 (fig. 38). This is closer in proportion to the early ships
than any of the other longships, but the fact that Skuldelev 5 is
relatively short means that it could not have been much narrower
and still had room for the crew and their equipment and stores. The
ship is built partly from new oak, but is completed on one side with
reused timbers of pine and ash from other ships. One of these is the
uppermost strake with the oar holes. This had previously been used
for the same purpose in a ship of a different size, so some of the
existing holes were blocked up and new ones cut instead. The ship
shows signs of repeated repairs and was heavily worn by the time it
was deliberately sunk.

In contrast to the high status of most of the other known warships, Skuldelev 5 may have been a *leiðangr* ship. *Leiðangr* is known from late twelfth- and thirteenth-century law codes in Denmark, Norway and Sweden, and was a system (with considerable variation between regions, as well as between kingdoms) whereby the king could summon ships and crews in wartime. The burden of supplying ships, men and provisions for such a fleet was distributed among all free landholders on the basis of territorial units. Land was divided into large areas responsible for one ship each and again into smaller units that had to provide one man with weapons and provisions. With thirteen rowing benches, Skuldelev 5 represents the lowest limit of the size of ship that could be supplied. The reuse of materials in the original construction and the ship's worn-out state are consistent with a levy ship built and maintained at minimum cost, rather than the warship of a chieftain.

This interpretation is not without problems, as the particular laws that support it come from western Norway, not Denmark and all the surviving law codes in any case date from well after the Viking Age. The earliest surviving reference to *leiðangr* in Denmark is from 1085, while Skuldelev 5 was built in *c.* 1030. Opinions are divided on how far back into the Viking Age some form of the *leiðangr* can be projected, but it is unlikely that the laws governing *leiðangr* remained completely the same between the early eleventh century and the late twelfth century, as this was also a period of wider changes in society and warfare. However, from 1018 to 1042 Denmark was under the rule of Cnut the Great and his sons, as was England (see p. 70). Given that England certainly had a ship levy system before this and that a clear Anglo-Saxon influence is visible in other aspects of Cnut's kingship in Denmark, he could have introduced a version of the *leiðangr* in Denmark before his death in 1035. The interpretation of Skuldelev 5 as a *leiðangr* ship thus remains a possibility, but not a certainty.

A final small warship worthy of mention comes from Puck, near Gdansk in Poland. The warship Puck 2 is around 20 metres long and dates from the first half of the tenth century. The Slavs who inhabited the southern coast of the Baltic had shipbuilding traditions of their own, including the fastening of the overlapping strakes with wooden trenails rather than rivets and using moss as caulking, and these features are found on the Puck ship. However, Slavic vessels typically stepped the mast on a specially constructed rib (running sideways across the ship) rather than on a keelson (running lengthways), while Puck 2 has a keelson similar to those found on Viking ships. The Baltic was very much a part of the Viking world, and had close links with southern Scandinavia through trade, as well as through political alliances and intermarriage. It is therefore unsurprising that a ship from the southern Baltic should combine elements from both Scandinavian and Slavic shipbuilding traditions.

WARSHIPS

Ship	Date	Length (m)	Breadth (m)	Length/ breadth ratio	Draught	No. of oars
Hedeby ship burial	c. 830–850	17.00–20.00	2.70–3.50	4.8– 7.4	Uncertain	Uncertain
Ladby	c. 900	21.54	2.92	7.40	1.05	30–32
Puck 2	900–950	c. 20.00	c. 2.20	c. 9.10	Uncertain	Uncertain
Hedeby 1	c. 985	30.90	2.70	11.40	1.50	c. 60
Roskilde 6	c. 1025	37.27	3.99	9.30	0.84	78–80
Skuldelev 5	c. 1030	17.30	2.47	7.00	1.16	26
Skuldelev 2	c. 1042	29.30	3.80	7.70	1.80	60

Large warships

Three large warships survive from the late Viking Age. The earliest of these, Hedeby 1, was around 31 metres long with an extremely narrow profile even by the standards of other longships (fig. 39). The ship was built *c.* 985, primarily from oak from the Hedeby area. It was constructed with particular care and skill, using planks of wood more than 10 metres long for the strakes. Fewer joints meant fewer weak points in the hull, and the joints between timbers are also more elaborate than in most ships, combining strength with a decorative effect. There are ornamental mouldings on many of the timbers and an unusually large number of rivets were used to connect the overlapping strakes, making these joints even more secure. The quality of construction and the substantial resources indicated by the choice of timber and the number of rivets point to the ship being commissioned by someone very wealthy. Since Hedeby was an important centre of royal authority as well as a major trading centre, it is likely that this was a royal warship. It ended up as a charred wreck in Hedeby harbour and while it may have been

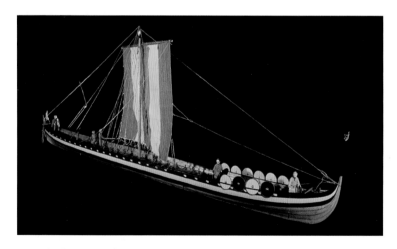

39. Scale model of the large warship, Hedeby 1. The original was around 31 m long.

Wikinger Museum Haithabu, Schleswig

40. The warship Skuldelev 2, *c.* 1042. The ship was built in the Dublin area, but found at Skuldelev, near Roskilde, Denmark.

Oak. L 29.3 m
Viking Ship Museum, Roskilde

41. The *Sea Stallion* from Glendalough, a reconstruction of the warship Skuldelev 2. The ship sailed in 2007 from Denmark to Ireland, where Skuldelev 2 was originally built.

deliberately sent into the harbour as a fire ship, it is possible that the damage was the result of an accidental fire.

Skuldelev 2 (fig. 40) is another warship of comparable size at around 30 metres long, but is broader than Hedeby 1. Like Hedeby 1, it had around thirty rowing benches, so required a crew of at least sixty, but the extra breadth as well as the space fore and aft meant that there was room for a full crew of around eighty. Like all of the warships, it carried both sail and oars, and experiments with a full-scale reconstruction, the *Sea Stallion* from Glendalough (fig. 41), have demonstrated that it was capable of performing well on the open sea: the *Sea Stallion* sailed from Roskilde to Dublin around Scotland in 2007 and back via the English Channel in 2008. This voyage tied in with the origins of the ship, which was built of oak from the Dublin area in 1042 and was repaired around twenty years later with oak also from the British Isles. Dublin was a major Viking settlement and the centre of a small kingdom. It had strong links with both native and Viking rulers elsewhere in Britain and Ireland and significant commercial connections with north-west England. The ship falls within the Scandinavian tradition, but with minor variations in form, which may reflect Anglo-Saxon or Irish influence.

The warship Roskilde 6

The longest Viking ship discovered so far was found almost by accident. The Viking Ship Museum at Roskilde is home to the five ships recovered at Skuldelev in the Roskilde Fjord (see p. 30). In addition to displaying and researching the ships themselves, the museum is a leader in the experimental reconstruction and sailing of Viking ships, and has built a small fleet, including versions of all of the Skuldelev ships. The museum is also home to a number of more recent historic ships and boats. In the 1990s, the decision was

42. The excavation of Roskilde 6 in 1997.

43. A section of Roskilde 6 assembled for display. Part of the keelson is visible, above the keel in the centre of the picture, together with the floor timbers reinforcing the strakes (planks) to either side of the keel.

made to create a museum 'island', with a harbour for the museum's ships, a shipyard for constructing more, plus additional facilities for education and conservation. The site was investigated archaeologically before construction began and in 1996–7 the remains of a further nine ships were excavated. These mostly date from after the Viking Age, but among them was a large warship from the early eleventh century, Roskilde 6 (fig. 42).

Since the ship was probably wrecked rather than deliberately sunk or buried, the upper parts were apparently salvaged, either to reuse the timbers or to prevent the ship from becoming a hazard to other ships. Both stems are missing, as are the upper strakes, frames and the mast. Nevertheless, what remains – around 20 per cent of the total hull – is hugely impressive. Most of the keel survives and at 32 metres it alone is longer than any other known Viking ship. In addition to the keel, a substantial section of the lower hull is present, together with part of the massive keelson. This supported the mast but also reinforced the keel, which was important in a ship of such great length. Within the hull, the floor timbers – the lower part of the frames – also survive (fig. 43). As the thwarts would have been placed directly above these, they therefore indicate the distance between the oar holes. There would have been space for thirty-nine to forty pairs of oars in total, compared with thirty pairs each in Skuldelev 2 and Hedeby 1.

Analysis of the surviving timbers shows that the ship was made from oak from south-eastern Norway between 1018 and 1032, probably c. 1025. It is likely that the ship was built in this area too, although it was repaired at least once elsewhere, since one of the planks was felled in the Baltic after 1039. It is unclear just how long after this the ship continued to be used before it finally sank at Roskilde. The date range for the original construction is intriguing, because it coincides with a key moment in the history of the region. Norway was ruled from 1015 to 1028 by Olaf Haraldsson (Saint Olaf, c. 995–1030), whose power base was in south-eastern Norway. For most of this period Denmark was ruled by Cnut the Great, who conquered England in 1016 and shortly afterwards became king of Denmark, which at this time included the southern part of what is now Sweden. In 1025, Cnut laid claim to Norway, which had at various times in the previous century fallen under Danish rule. Olaf resisted Cnut's claims, but was defeated at the

44. Roskilde 6 on display at the National Museum of Denmark, 2013. The stem and stern are each around 5 metres high. As the originals do not survive, the size and shape has been calculated by comparison with other examples.

battle of Helgeå in 1025 or 1026 and forced into exile in 1028. He returned to Norway in 1030 in an unsuccessful attempt to reclaim his kingdom, only to be killed at the battle of Stiklestad. Norway was ruled from 1028 by Cnut's young son Svein (c. 1016–35), with his English mother Ælfgifu (c. 990–after 1040) as regent. However, Svein's kingship proved to be no more popular in Norway than Olaf's. Following Cnut's death in 1035, Olaf's son, Magnus the Good (c. 1024–47), was able to recover the Norwegian throne and from 1042 to 1047 he also took control of Denmark, although not without resistance.

The scale of Roskilde 6 (fig. 44) means that the ship must have been commissioned by someone extremely important. As discussed above, a longship of thirty-nine to forty rowing benches is massive by the standards of written evidence – there are few references to ships above twenty-five benches – as well as compared with other surviving Viking ships. It is likely that even if Roskilde 6 was not a king's ship, it was built by royal command, as not many other individuals could have commanded the necessary manpower and resources. The ship was made in the heartland of Olaf's power, possibly to assist in extending his own royal authority or to resist the expansion of Cnut's influence. However, the imprecision of the ship's dating means that it could have been built for Cnut, or even for Svein, providing an impressive reminder for anyone who saw her of Danish authority over the valuable timber resources of southern Norway. Equally, by the time that the ship was sunk near the important Danish royal centre of Roskilde, Denmark may well have been under the rule of the Norwegian Magnus. Whatever the story, the ship today symbolizes royal power at the height of the Viking Age in the early eleventh century (fig. 45).

Cargo ships

Oft he sailed
To Semigallia
In splendid knarr
Round Domesnes

Runic inscription from Mervalla, Södermanland, Sweden, 11th century

Trade was one of the driving forces behind the Scandinavian expansion overseas in the Viking Age. Ribe in western Denmark and Helgö in eastern Sweden were established as important trading centres even before the Viking Age. Other centres for long-distance trade – Hedeby, Birka and Kaupang – emerged in the ninth century, with the development of larger towns in all three Nordic kingdoms in the late tenth and eleventh centuries, along with many smaller trading places (fig. 46). The growth of a vast network of long-distance and local trade created a need for ships with the capacity to carry cargo. At the same time, the colonization of the North Atlantic required sea-going vessels that could supply the settlements on the Faeroes, Iceland and Greenland with timber, livestock and other necessities, as well as transporting the settlers themselves.

46. Major maritime and riverine sailing routes providing trading connections between the Viking homelands and the North Atlantic, the Mediterranean and the Middle East, and Central Asia.

Small cargo ships

Not all cargo ships were particularly large, reflecting the various demands of different types of traffic. Skuldelev 6, built of pine in

NORTH
SEA

BALTIC SEA

MEDITERRANEAN SEA

BLACK SEA

Kaupang

Birka Helgö

Staraya Ladoga

Novgorod

Jaroslavl

Pskov

Ribe

Gnezdovo
Smolensk

Hedeby

Wolin

Janow Pomorski

York

Chernigov

Dublin

Chester

Kiev

Limerick

London

Dorestad

Rome

Constantinople

Cordoba

Trent

Thames

Rhine

Elbe

Vistula

Pripets

Seine

Loire

Dniester

Danube

Dvina

Volkhov

Velikaja

Lovat

Dnieper

Sula

Don

Donets

Dnieper

Oka

47. The small cargo ship
Skuldelev 6, *c.* 1030.

Pine. L 11.2 m
Viking Ship Museum, Roskilde

western Norway *c.* 1030, is only 11.2 metres long, which is smaller than any of the warships discussed here, and was designed to carry a sail, although there was originally also capacity for perhaps six oars on either side. The ship was later made taller and the number of oars was probably reduced. The shallow draft meant that the ship could land almost anywhere and in its initial form it was a highly versatile vessel for use in coastal waters. The conversion seems to have turned Skuldelev 6 (fig. 47) into a more limited, or perhaps more specialized, small cargo ship.

In contrast, Skuldelev 3 (fig. 48) was designed as a cargo ship from the outset. Built of oak in Denmark *c.* 1040, it is 14 metres long and is comparatively low and slender, with only a few oar holes for manoeuvring and a sail as the main means of propulsion. Skuldelev 3 would have had a capacity of around 4 to 5 tonnes and, like Skuldelev 6, it is likely to have been used primarily in coastal waters for small-scale trading.

The Äskekärr ship was found in a marshy area adjacent to the River Göta, in western Sweden, upstream from modern Göteberg (Gothenberg). The Göta in the late Viking Age formed the border between the emerging kingdoms of Denmark, Norway and Sweden. The ship was built of local oak around the late tenth century. Only the lower parts of the ship survive (see fig. 20, p. 32), including the 13-metre keel and the bottom sections of the stems, and from these a total length of around 16 metres can be estimated. It is uncertain how many oars the ship carried, but it was definitely designed to sail, as the keelson is present. This is more roughly made than the rest of the ship and is dated about sixty years later than the other timbers. Therefore, it may have been a replacement for the original, which was presumably damaged.

48. The cargo ship Skuldelev 3, *c.* 1040.

Pine. L 14 m
Viking Ship Museum, Roskilde

49. The Klåstad ship, late 10th century. The ship capsized and its uneven position in the ground meant that one side was preserved and the other not.

Oak, pine and beech. L *c.* 20 m
Slottsfjellmuseum, Tønsberg

The Klåstad ship (fig. 49) also dates from the late tenth century and sank *c.* 1000 with a cargo of whetstones from Eidsborg, southern Norway. Whetstones of Norwegian schist were a major export and have been found in many of the Viking settlements overseas as well as around Scandinavia. Like the Äskekärr ship it was designed for cargo. The majority of the hull was oak, with some elements made of pine and beech. As only part of the ship survives, the dimensions are not precise. It is estimated that it was a little over 20 metres long – slightly shorter than the Oseberg ship (see pp. 48–51), but deeper in proportion to its length and breadth.

Large cargo ships

Skuldelev 1 was built of pine in western Norway c. 1030 and was repaired with oak planks on at least three occasions, including two using oak from southern Scandinavia. Although at 16.5 metres long the ship is shorter than the Klåstad ship or the general purpose vessels, the hull is comparatively deep and broad (fig. 50), giving a carrying capacity of up to 25 tonnes, with a half deck fore and aft, and open amidships. As with Skuldelev 3, the only oars were for manoeuvring and the sail was the main method of propulsion. The deep, heavy Skuldelev 1 would not have had the flexibility to land just anywhere, especially with cargo aboard, but would have needed to dock alongside jetties like those found at trading centres such as Dorestad and Hedeby. These centres were established before any of the surviving large cargo ships, so it is possible that similar vessels existed at an earlier date as well. Skuldelev 1 has been identified as a cargo ship intended primarily for use on the route between western Norway and the Baltic, but sailing trials of two reconstructions of this ship, *Saga Siglar* and *Ottar* (fig. 51), have shown that the ship was perfectly capable of crossing the North Sea, or even the Atlantic.

An even larger cargo ship was discovered in the harbour at Hedeby in 1981. Only parts of the vessel Hedeby 3 have been recovered, but others have been recorded *in situ*, permitting a detailed reconstruction of some sections and an estimate of the overall size. The ship was around 22 metres long, with a design and relative proportions comparable to Skuldelev 1. On this basis, it seems likely that the ship had a capacity of up to 60 tonnes of cargo. A ship of these dimensions would certainly have been capable of crossing the North Sea or the Atlantic and its existence demonstrates clearly the scale of trade in the late Viking Age. Although rather larger than Skuldelev 1, Hedeby 3 is slightly earlier, being built c. 1025 in the Hedeby area, primarily of oak.

50. Interior view of Skuldelev 1, *c.* 1030. The deep sides and comparative breadth of Skuldelev 1 leave no doubt that this is a purpose-built cargo ship.

Pine, oak. L 16.5 m
Viking Ship Museum, Roskilde

CARGO SHIPS

Ship	Date	Length (m)	Breadth (m)	Length/breadth ratio	Draught	Cargo capacity (tonnes)
Klåstad	Late 10th century	c. 20.0	c. 4.5	c. 4.44	Uncertain	Uncertain
Äskekärr	Late 10th century	c. 16.0	c. 4.0	c. 4.00	Uncertain	Uncertain
Skuldelev 6	c. 1030	11.2	2.50	4.48	0.50	Uncertain
Skuldelev 3	c. 1040	14.0	3.30	4.24	0.85	4–5
Skuldelev 1	c. 1030	16.5	4.80	3.44	1.20	c. 25
Hedeby 3	c. 1025	c. 22.0	6.20	3.55	Uncertain	c. 60

51. The *Ottar*, a reconstruction of the cargo ship Skuldelev 1. The ship is designed to be sailed rather than rowed, and can be handled by a small crew, maximizing the space available for cargo.

52. Reconstruction of the central section of the post-Viking cargo ship from Bryggen, Norway, *c.* 1188.

Pine. L *c.* 30 m, W *c.* 9 m
Bryggens Museum, Bergen

Several large cargo ships survive from the eleventh and twelfth centuries, and the culmination of this type of ship can be seen in one from *c.* 1188, which was recovered from the medieval harbour of Bryggen (Bergen) in Norway. The ship is only partially preserved, but the remaining elements show that it was massive (fig. 52), around 9 metres wide and probably 30 metres long, with a total cargo capacity of about 120 tonnes. It was built in the same Scandinavian clinker-built tradition as the various ships of the Viking Age discussed previously, but its huge size, together with the weight of the cargo, necessitated a much more solid construction and substantial internal frames, while its depth meant that it required a proper harbour as it would be too heavy to be moved easily if beached. For all their similarities to earlier ships, vessels such as the Bryggen ship lack the flexibility of hull and function of true Viking ships.

Epilogue

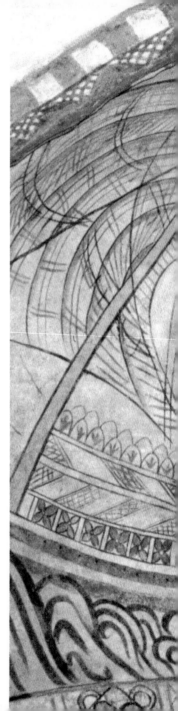

There at the quayside was the ship which Jon had built for the Earl. It had thirty-five rowing benches, and was remarkably well-constructed, and carved everywhere, and all inlaid with gold on the stems and the wind vanes ... The ship was the most expensive of its kind.

Orkneyinga saga, anonymous, *c.* 1200

The Viking Age is generally seen as ending in the late eleventh century, but the building of ships of Viking type did not simply stop at this point. Large ships in the same tradition continued to be built in the twelfth and thirteenth centuries, although they faced increasing competition from other ship types, especially the cog (fig. 53, opposite), which became widespread across northern Europe in the later Middle Ages. In addition to cargo ships like the Bryggen ship, sagas of the late twelfth and thirteenth centuries suggest that longships became higher and wider, if not necessarily longer, in order to carry more crew. Large warships must also have required a stronger and heavier structure than earlier ships. This may have been a factor that led to the declining popularity of ships in the Viking tradition in favour of the cog. The Viking ships required very substantial timbers, including long straight trunks for the keel, mast, keelson and strakes, and trees of exactly the right shape for elements such as stems, ribs and knees (see pp. 34–8). As the

ships became bigger, it became difficult to find enough trees of the correct size, so practical considerations as well as fashion may have contributed to the shift to other ship types.

The Viking ship tradition did not disappear entirely, either in Scandinavia or in the Viking settlements overseas. In the Western Isles of Scotland, which had been settled by the Vikings and remained under Norwegian rule until 1266, smaller warships continued in use into the sixteenth century. The larger galleys seem to have been comparable in size with smaller warships such as Ladby and Skuldelev 5, which were ideal for amphibious warfare in shallow island waters. Such ships were often pictured on memorial

53. (previous page) Wall painting in the parish church at Skamstrup in Denmark, 14th century. The picture shows St Olaf defeating his half-brother in a race despite pausing for a church service before sailing. It has been suggested that the miraculous nature of his victory is highlighted by the fact that Olaf is in a heavier cog, while Harald has a traditional longship, which might be expected to be faster.

54. Detail of the tombstone of Alasdair Crotach McLeod at St Clement's Church, Rodel Harris, 1528. Despite its late date, the ship remains firmly in the Viking shipbuilding tradition, except that the steering oar has been replaced by the stern rudder typical of the later medieval period.

55. Four men rowing a 'sixern', or 'sixareen', 1920s–1930s. The sixern is typical of the fishing boats of Shetland in the late 19th–early 20th century, but visibly still related to its prototypes in the Viking Age.

Shetland Museum and Archives

stones, sometimes in considerable detail, and while the steering oar has been replaced by a stern rudder, requiring a stern of a different shape, the form of the ship and rigging is otherwise closely reminiscent of the Viking ships (fig. 54). Moving further down the scale, fishing boats in Scandinavia and Scotland long retained elements of lines and building techniques dating back to the Viking Age. The main fishing boat of Shetland up to the late nineteenth century was the sixern, a name derived from the Old Norse *sexaering*, meaning six-oared boat (fig. 55), while boats of traditional design have never entirely disappeared in Scandinavia.

Our understanding of Viking ships has been massively enhanced by experimentation in the reconstruction and sailing of vessels based on the archaeological remains of those from the ninth to the eleventh centuries discussed here. The success of such experiments has in part been due to the survival of later boats in the same tradition and even more to the fact that, when the first experiments began, there were still boatbuilders in Denmark and Norway with enough understanding of traditional boatbuilding to advise on and participate in the process. With the combination of modern archaeological science and craft skills handed down from the Vikings, an ever increasing number of Viking ships and boats are sailing once more (fig. 56).

56. A reconstruction based on the Oseberg ship, but with two additional strakes on either side, giving the ship much more height amidships, and thereby making the ship more seaworthy in bad weather.

Seeing Viking ships today

Viking Ship Museum (Oslo, Norway)

The Viking Ship Museum in Oslo houses the material from the ship burials of Gokstad, Oseberg and Tune. The two ships from Gokstad and Oseberg, which are the most complete of all the surviving ships, are on permanent display, together with the remains of the less well-preserved ship from Tune and two of the three rowing boats from the Gokstad ship burial. The display also includes the grave goods from Gokstad and Oseberg.

Viking Ship Museum (Roskilde, Denmark)

The Viking Ship Museum at Roskilde houses the largest collection of original Viking ships in the world, including the five Skuldelev ships. All of these survive only partially, but the display indicates clearly the shape of the missing components. The museum also has permanent displays about Viking ships, thematic temporary exhibitions, a boatyard for building reconstructions of Viking ships and boats, a conservation laboratory, educational facilities and a harbour with fully functional reconstructions of the Skuldelev ships.

Viking Museum (Ladby, Denmark)

The Viking Museum at Ladby has been built around the Ladby Viking warship, preserving the burial *in situ* and suggesting the atmosphere of a burial chamber. The display also includes some of the grave goods from the burial; others are on display in the National Museum of Denmark in Copenhagen.

Göteborg City Museum (Göteborg, Sweden)

The permanent display in the Göteborg City Museum includes the remains of the Äskekärr cargo ship, which at the time of writing is the only surviving ship from the Viking Age on public display in Sweden.

Slottsfjellmuseum (Tønsberg, Norway)

The remains of the wreck of the trading ship from nearby Klåstad are on permanent display at the Slottsfjellmuseum, Tønsberg. Tønsberg is also the permanent home of a recently completed functional reconstruction of the Oseberg ship. There are plans to build a working reconstruction of the Klåstad ship.

Wikinger Museum Haithabu and Archäologisches Landesmuseum, Schloss Gottorf (Schleswig, Germany)

The Wikinger Museum Haithabu near Schleswig houses the remains of the large warship excavated from the harbour area in Hedeby (Haithabu). Some of these are on view, accompanied by a fully reconstructed section to set the original remains in context. The display also includes treasures from the Hedeby ship burial. The Archäologisches Landesmuseum in nearby Schleswig houses the Nydam boat, together with a log boat and other finds from the same site.

National Museum of Ireland (Dublin, Ireland)

Although the National Museum of Ireland does not have any complete ships, it has a collection of ship parts from Viking Dublin. Several of these form a display on Viking shipbuilding, together with a full-sized reconstruction of one of the smaller boats from the Gokstad burial.

National Museums of Scotland (Edinburgh, Scotland)

The National Museums of Scotland do not have any complete ships, but their display includes two ship stems from the Viking Age that were deposited in a bog on the island of Eigg to season the timber. The Vikings displays also contain grave goods from a boat burial at Kiloran Bay, Colonsay.

Further reading

J. Bill, S. Nielsen, E. Andersen and T. Damgård-Sørensen, *Welcome on Board! The Sea Stallion from Glendalough. A Viking Longship Recreated* (Roskilde 2007)

J. Borg, M. Gustafsson and M. Sjölin, *The Story of the Viking-Age Ship from Äskekärr* (Göteborg 2000)

S. Brink with N. Price (eds), *The Viking World* (London and New York 2008)

A.W. Brøgger and H. Shetelig, *Viking Ships: Their Ancestry and Evolution* (Revised edition, Oslo 1971).

O. Crumlin-Pedersen (ed.), *Aspects of Maritime Scandinavia, AD 200–1200* (Roskilde 1991)

O. Crumlin-Pedersen, *Viking-Age Ships and Shipbuilding in Hedeby/Haithabu and Schleswig*. Ships and Boats of the North 2 (Schleswig/Roskilde 1997)

O. Crumlin-Pedersen, *Archaeology and the Sea in Scandinavia and Britain*: *A personal account* (Roskilde 2010)

O. Crumlin-Pedersen and O. Olsen (eds), *The Skuldelev Ships I. Topography, Archaeology, History, Conservation and Display*. Ships and Boats of the North 4.1 (Roskilde 2002)

O. Crumlin-Pedersen and B. Munch Thye (eds), *The Ship as Symbol in Prehistoric and Medieval Scandinavia* (Copenhagen 1995)

O. Crumlin-Pedersen and M. Vinner (eds), *Sailing into the Past. Proceedings of the International Seminar on Replicas of Ancient and Medieval Vessels* (Roskilde 1986)

R. Hall, *Exploring the World of the Vikings* (London 2007)

J. Jesch, *Ships and Men in the Late Viking Age: the Vocabulary of Runic Inscriptions and Skaldic Verse* (London 2001)

G. Larsson, *Ship and Society: Maritime Ideology in Late Iron Age Sweden* (Uppsala 2007)

G.J. Marcus, *The Conquest of the North Atlantic* (Woodbridge 1990)

E. Nylén and J.P. Lamm, *Stones, Ships and Symbols* (Stockholm 1988)

A. Nørgård Jørgensen, J. Pind, L. Jørgensen and B. Clausen (eds), *Maritime Warfare in Northern Europe. Technology, Organisation, Logistics and Administration 500 BC–1500 AD* (Copenhagen 2002)

O. Olsen, J. Skamby Madsen and F. Rieck (eds), *Shipshape – Essays for Ole Crumlin-Pedersen* (Roskilde 1995)

D. Rixson, *The West Highland Galley* (Edinburgh 1998)

T. Sjøvold, *The Viking Ships in Oslo* (Oslo 1985)

A.C. Sørensen, *Ladby, A Danish Ship-Grave from the Viking Age*. Ships and Boats of the North 3 (Roskilde 2001)

G. Williams, P. Pentz and M. Wemhoff (eds), *Vikings: life and legend* (London 2014)

Illustration credits

The publisher would like to thank the copyright holders for granting permission to reproduce the images illustrated. Every attempt has been made to trace accurate ownership of copyrighted images in this book. Errors and omissions will be corrected in subsequent editions provided notification is sent to the publisher.

All photographs of British Museum objects are © The Trustees of the British Museum, courtesy of the Department of Photography and Imaging.

Frontispiece: Brooch, 800–1050. Tjørnehoj II, Fyn, Denmark. Copper alloy. L 5.5 cm
© The National Museum of Denmark

Fig. 1 © Costa/Leemage / The Bridgeman Art Library
Fig. 2 Copyright unknown
Fig. 3 © Robert Harding Picture Library / SuperStock
Fig. 4 coin © Norges Bank; stamp © Norway Post
Fig. 5 1979,1039.18 © Bureau of Engraving and Printing, Peking. Photo © The Trustees of the British Museum
Fig. 6 © Norwegian Canning Museum
Fig. 7 © Jaguar Land Rover Limited
Fig. 8 © Sweden, Europe, True Colour Satellite Image With Border / Planet Observer / UIG / The Bridgeman Art Library

Fig. 9 © National Museum of Ireland
Fig. 10 © The National Museum of Denmark
Fig. 11 © De Agostini Picture Library / G. Dagli Orti / The Bridgeman Art Library
Fig. 12 Photo © Vikingemuseet Ladby
Fig. 13 © Robert Harding Picture Library / SuperStock
Fig. 14 © Jeff J. Mitchell / Reuters / Corbis
Fig. 15 © Museum of Cultural History, University of Oslo / Eirik Irgens Johnsen
Fig. 16 © Museum of Cultural History, University of Oslo
Fig. 17 © The Ardnamurchan Transitions Project
Fig. 18 © Pieta Greaves, AOC Archaeology and the Ardnamurchan Transitions Project
Fig. 19 © The Viking Ship Museum, Denmark.
Fig. 20 © Göteborgs Stadsmuseum Bilder
Fig. 21 Paul Goodhead © The Trustees of the British Museum
Fig. 22 Paul Goodhead © The Trustees of the British Museum
Fig. 23 © National Museums Scotland
Fig. 24 1891,1021.87 © The Trustees of the British Museum
Fig. 25 Paul Goodhead © The Trustees of the British Museum
Fig. 26 © The National Museum of Denmark
Fig. 27 © The National Museum of Denmark

Fig. 28 1938,0202.1 © The Trustees of
the British Museum
Fig. 29 © The Trustees of the British Museum
Fig. 30 © Museum of Cultural History,
University of Oslo / Ellen C. Holte
Fig. 31 © Werner Forman Archive/ Maritime
Museum, Bergen
Fig. 32 © Museum of Cultural History,
University of Oslo / Eirik Irgens Johnsen
Fig. 33 © Museum of Cultural History,
University of Oslo / Eirik Irgens Johnsen
Fig. 34 © Museum of Cultural History,
University of Oslo / Eirik Irgens Johnsen
Fig. 35 © Museum of Cultural History,
University of Oslo / Eirik Irgens Johnsen
Fig. 36 Paul Goodhead © The Trustees of
the British Museum
Fig. 37 iron curls © Vikingemuseet Ladby; dragon
mould © National Historical Museum Stockholm
Fig. 38 © The Viking Ship Museum, Denmark.
Photo: Photography and Imaging, The British Museum
Fig. 39 © Wikinger Museum Haithabu
Fig. 40 © The Viking Ship Museum, Denmark.
Photo: Photography and Imaging, The British Museum
Fig. 41 © The Viking Ship Museum, Denmark.
Photo: Werner Karrasch.

Fig. 42 © The Viking Ship Museum, Denmark.
Photo: Werner Karrasch.
Fig. 43 © The Viking Ship Museum, Denmark.
Photo: Photography and Imaging, The British Museum
Fig. 44 © The National Museum of Denmark.
Photo: Photography and Imaging, The British Museum
Fig. 45 © The National Museum of Denmark.
Photo: Photography and Imaging, The British Museum
Fig. 46 Paul Goodhead © The Trustees of
the British Museum
Fig. 47 © The Viking Ship Museum, Denmark.
Photo: Photography and Imaging, The British Museum
Fig. 48 © The Viking Ship Museum, Denmark.
Photo: Photography and Imaging, The British Museum
Fig. 49 © Slottsfjellsmuseet
Fig. 50 © The Viking Ship Museum, Denmark.
Photo: Photography and Imaging, The British Museum
Fig. 51 © The Viking Ship Museum, Denmark
Fig. 52 © Bryggens Museum, Bergen
Fig. 53 © The National Museum of Denmark
Fig. 54 © RCAHMS
Fig. 55 © Shetland Museum and Archives
Fig. 56 © Robert Harding Picture Library / SuperStock

Acknowledgements

The author would like to thank Claudia Bloch, Senior Development Editor
at The British Museum Press, for seeing the book through to publication;
Thomas J.T. Williams, who commented on the publication in draft;
Paul Goodhead for the illustrations; Katherine Anderson, Picture Researcher,
and Kate Oliver, Senior Production Controller at The British Museum Press;
and Paul Palmer-Edwards of Grade Design.

Particular thanks are also due to Kristiane Strætkvern and her colleagues
for their invaluable work on the interpretation and conservation of Roskilde 6,
and to the various colleagues who have shared their expertise on the subject
of Viking ships and related subjects over many years, especially Jan Bill, Niels
Lund and the late Ole Crumlin-Pedersen.